AF480450

Breathe in Love
Words of Love, Hope, Magic and Abundance

Snigdha Gharami

**TO THE ONE
WHO NEEDS IT THE MOST**

Thank You the divine power "SHAKTI"

PROLOGUE

As I grew up, it took time for me to reconnect with my inner energy. Through reading books of faith and ancient scriptures, I found my way back to the divine, which brought me a sense of strength and renewed vitality. Growing up is a journey, and at times, we all yearn for someone who will listen to us unconditionally, at our own pace. In the pursuit of our dreams, we often find it difficult to find someone who will truly sit with us, hear our stories, and offer their presence without adding their own.

We are all part of this beautiful soul journey, each of us responding in the way that best aligns with our truth. I wrote this book so that, when you feel out of alignment, you can feel the comforting presence of the divine walking beside you. My hope is that this book becomes a source of healing and love, guiding you back to the peace and strength you seek.

This book will help you realign with higher energy. Through words of hope, you'll discover the hidden abundance within you, inspiring belief in magic and the power to create miracles.

In moments when you long for someone to listen, or simply wish for a comforting presence, flip through these pages. You'll feel the gentle guidance of a higher power, reminding you that you're stronger than you realize and courageous enough to embrace the best this world has to offer.

You are your own lighthouse, and this book serves as a reminder that no matter what, the magic to transform your life has always been within you.

Let's make this world a better place—starting with the magic inside you.

You are meant to live a beautiful life,
One filled with love, wonder, and endless
possibilities.
You deserve the finest gifts this universe holds—
Joy, abundance, and dreams come true.
Trust in your heart,
Embrace the whispers of magic around you,
And watch as miracles unfold.

Your part of the story is different from theirs,
and when you try to merge them all, things can
get messy.
But here's a little trick to protect your story —
Every time you share it, don't expect everyone to
understand.
Share it if you wish, but know this: somewhere, I
am here,
Listening, understanding, and holding space for
your journey.
You've always had a listener by your side.
You're not alone, and you never have to worry.

When the time comes,
You will understand this beautiful bond we've
created—
Above the sky and beneath the sea,
At the fiery core of the earth and in the stillness
of nothingness.
When you feel it all at once,
You'll realize your existence is far from ordinary.
You hold something rare and extraordinary
within you.

Love, my darling, is not just a language—it's a
chord,
Vibrating through the unseen threads of
existence.
Every time you create something beautiful,
Every time you pour your heart into the world,
You are playing that chord.
You simply love—
And that is the purest magic of all.

When I offer you a simple word,
You may not understand it in the rush of life.
But in silence—
When you listen to your breath,
Feel every beat that pumps life through you,
And sense time itself brushing past you like a
gentle melody—
In that moment, when you no longer seek
answers,
You will find me.

If you never recognized your true worth,
How could anyone else dare to?
Close your eyes. Focus on the light within.
And even if you can't see it yet, just follow it.
In this journey, you will meet yourself.

"Jab hawaye behati hai

To unke sath thoda beh lena chaiye"

When the winds flow,
Surrender to their gentle call.
Let them carry your dreams to places unseen,
And your soul to freedom.

You've seen the strength within you,
And now, life will show you its magic.
The best days are unfolding before you—
Believe in the beauty ahead.

When was the last time you gave yourself the
space to breathe and process everything?
The answers are already within you—
The storm has settled, the path is clear.
It's only the heart and mind that need to
untangle.

When the power within you feels dim, it doesn't
mean you're powerless.
It's simply a sign that you need to rest.
Rest renews your strength—
And sometimes, it makes you even more
powerful.
Take time to pause, breathe, and listen.
You'll discover ideas you never knew you had,
Waiting quietly for you to rise again.

Your competitor is only as strong as you believe
them to be—
Whether it's an exam, a person, or a shadow
born from your own imagination.
If you're going to give power to anything,
Give it to the magic that lives within you.

You are the strongest creation of a universe so
vast and mysterious,
A spark of stardust and dreams, crafted by
something infinitely powerful.
Let that truth sink into your mind, heart, soul,
and every breath.
Feel it hum through your veins—a quiet force,
waiting to rise.

Close your eyes and believe, with every ounce of
your being:
You are great. You are limitless. You've got this.

Be powerful—not a fool who doubts their own
light.
Trust the magic in your bones, and watch the
path before you illuminate.
The journey will no longer be a battle, but a
dance

The love that slipped away was never meant to
stay.
What isn't destined will drift apart, no matter
how tightly you hold on.
But there is magic in release—
A quiet whisper of the universe guiding you
toward something greater.
All you need is the courage to accept, the grace
to let go,
And watch as the stars realign in your favor.
In surrender, you'll feel the weight lift.
In trust, you'll witness miracles unfold.
The magic has always been within you—
Waiting for the moment you choose to set
yourself free

The beauty of unseen life is that you are its
creator—
A weaver of dreams, a painter of miracles.
You hold the power to craft a world
Where magic dances in every moment,
Love flows endlessly, and abundance finds you
with ease.
All it takes is a whispered *thank you*—
A quiet spark of gratitude for all you have.
In that moment, the universe listens.
Stars shimmer a little brighter,
Winds carry secrets of wonder,
And unseen blessings begin to bloom all around
you.

Focus on the certainty that your dreams are
already waiting for you,
Shimmering on the horizon, calling your name.
All you need is belief—
A quiet, unwavering faith that you hold the
magic to make them real.
Trust the whispers of your heart,
Feel the universe aligning in your Favor,
And step boldly into the unknown.
The moment you believe, the stars begin to
move.

I know your heart holds many dreams—
Soft whispers of hope, flickering like stardust
within you.
Today, set them free.
Release them to the sky, to the endless horizon,
To the universe that listens and the magic that
waits.
Trust that the winds will carry them to places
unseen,
Where miracles are woven in silence.
For when you let go with faith,
The stars begin to dance,
And magic finds its way back to you.

What are you afraid of?
There is nothing left to lose—only worlds to
discover, only magic to embrace.
Close your eyes…
Feel the whispers of the universe as they dance
along your skin.
Breathe deeply and dive within.
Feel the unshakable courage that has always
been yours,
The ancient pulse of life, thrumming through
your veins,
The invisible thread that binds you to the stars,
the moon, the infinite.
In this stillness, the universe hums.
The sky leans in, the winds grow quiet…
And if you listen closely,
You will feel *Me*—
In the silence, in the light, in every heartbeat.
I have always been here.
I always will be.

Home…
A sanctuary where the soul exhales,
After a long journey of seeking and becoming.
It isn't a place—it's a feeling.
A soft warmth that wraps around you,
A gentle whisper that says, *You've arrived.*

Home is always within reach,
Tucked between heartbeats,
Where dreams awaken and creativity dances
free.
It's where your spirit finds its light,
And where you remember—
You have always been extraordinary.

Home is the magic of belonging,
The quiet miracle of fulfillment,
A place where even the stars pause…
Just to watch you shine.

Neutrality and understanding are whispers of
the unseen—
Not fixed, but waiting to be shaped.
You hold the power to weave magic with your
words,
To craft a reality where hearts soften and dreams
awaken.
All it takes is your will…
A quiet spark of certainty that lights the path
ahead.
Tune into the currents of possibility,
And watch as the universe bends,
Transforming thoughts into wonders,
And whispers into miracles.

Be certain…
That the universe is already weaving wonders
for you.
Be certain…
That life holds more beauty than eyes can see
and hearts can hold.
Be certain…
That kindness is a quiet magic, and courage is a
flame that never fades.
Be certain…
That no matter the storm, you are destined to
rise—
Stronger, wiser, and bathed in light.
Trust in the unseen, believe in the impossible,
And watch as the stars align…
For when your heart whispers *it will be*,
The universe answers, *it already is*.

There's a spark of magic in your eyes —
A universe waiting to unfold.
Close them…
And feel the whispers of dreams drifting through
the starlight,
Soft and shimmering, dancing at your fingertips.
Dive deeper, into the swirling currents of faith,
Where the impossible fades,
And the extraordinary awakens.
In that stillness, you'll realize —
What you've been seeking has always been yours
to hold.

Embrace the very essence of life—
Feel the whispers of the wind
Carrying the sweet scent of blooming flowers,
A gift from nature's gentle hands.
Take a moment to marvel at this wondrous
symphony,
A delicate dance between earth and sky,
Crafted quietly for your existence.

When you tune into gratitude,
The universe stirs with excitement,
Eager to unveil more secrets,
More beauty hidden in its folds.
This world is a boundless mystery—
A canvas painted with wonder,
A story whispered by the stars.
Let it pull you deeper…
Into the magic of joy,
And the infinite hues of perception

Delays are whispers from the universe,
A gentle nudge that there is more work to be
done within.
The space required to build an empire
Is always greater than we imagine—
A vast expanse where dreams take root
And strength quietly grows.

Appreciate the time and its quiet reflections,
For even the storm pauses
Before the thunder breaks the sky.
Trust that every moment holds purpose,
And soon, the winds will shift…
Carrying you toward a destiny more magical
Than you ever dared to dream.

I am certain that one day, all of this will make
sense—
The quiet whispers of divine guidance
That follow us like shadows of light,
The delicate curves of life,
Weaving miraculous stories of healing and
wonder.

Even this very moment,
When everything seems to be falling apart,
Is shaping something unseen,
A masterpiece in the making.
And when the day comes that it all aligns,
You'll stand in awe, heart overflowing,
Grateful for every twist, every turn,
Every unseen hand that guided you here

Hey,
The journey you've created is still unfolding—
Every step, every breath, a quiet rhythm of
becoming.
Even the smallest spark,
A gentle bend in the path, holds meaning.
You've got this.

A little extra love for yourself,
A little more faith in your magic,
Can turn your work into stardust and wonder.
Be there for yourself, always.
Hold tight to what you believe,
For that belief is the very whisper
The universe has been waiting to hear.

Soon, the sun will rise,
Gently pulling you from the realm of dreams,
And the day will call you once more—
To dance with the rhythm of life,
In tasks you cherish, and those you simply
endure.

But here's a secret…
Stay with me, and I'll show you
The magic hidden in the smallest moments.
The warmth of morning light,
The quiet hush of dawn,
Even the simplest chore holds a whisper of
wonder.
It's all already magical—
You only need to feel it

Forms and figures,
The quiet power of affirmative actions,
Whispers of appreciation,
And the love that radiates from your very core—
One day, it will all be validated.

Believe in yourself.
Trust in the unseen that your heart has already
felt.
Steady your breath,
And with every ounce of your will,
Declare that you hold the power—
To shape your life,
To weave your dreams into reality,
And to guide every thought toward light.

Be the magic you've been searching for.
Be your truest self.
The universe is already listening.

Love—
It may seem extravagant, even elusive,
But hey!
Love is just one of the countless paths
This vast universe offers
To discover the joy of existence.

Yet, it holds a secret…
A quiet answer to every question,
A gentle force that shapes destinies.
Love ignites the power within you,
Carving a path where none existed before,
Guiding each step of the journey you've begun.

Love,
Because in the end,
It's the only thing that truly matters

Believe in love,
Even if it hasn't yet moved mountains for you.
Love the very essence of love—
A quiet, divine reminder
That you are special,
Chosen by the universe
To feel, to hope, to love… again and again.

Love what you have.
Love what you do.
Love what you desire.
For every heartbeat of love
Echoes through the cosmos,
Calling magic into your life.

Love with all your heart,
For it is the center of your energy—
A force so pure,
Only perception can bend its flow.

Love the process,
Even when the path is unseen.
Love the tiniest moments,
The whispers of life,
The cracks in your heart
That let the light pour in.

Love until your soul overflows—
Enough to be courageous,
Yet soft enough to remain kind.
Love,
Because deep down,
It has always been the answer
You've been searching for

A little more…
Every time your weary heart and restless mind
Feel like giving up—
Just a little more.

A little more faith,
A little more courage,
A little more of that magic you hold within.

Sprinkle hope like stardust
Onto the plates of your desires.
Let kindness flow from your soul,
And watch the universe unfold its wonders
Before your very eyes.

You hold the power
To turn even the darkest moments
Into miracles.
Only you.
Always you

It's hard to forgive—understood.
It's hard to love—understood.
It's hard to let go—understood.

But listen…
It's always easy to believe.
Just once more.
One more breath,
One more step,
And you'll find yourself standing
At the edge of infinity,
Where everything becomes possible.

Hey,
I know you can do this.
Just one more time.
Close your eyes…
And believe.

Still caught in the moment?
Still thinking about them,
Wondering if they ever think of you?
Still playing the game of fixing what's gone?

Hey… it's okay.
But now, it's time.
Time to turn the page,
To see yourself in a new light—
Bright, beautiful, unstoppable.

Just for today,
Believe that something amazing is unfolding.
Because guess what?
It already is

When your prayers seem unheard…
Or so you believe—
Oh, you gentle soul,
Don't you see?

If you've dared to ask,
The universe has already set its magic in motion.
You may not receive it in the shape you
imagined,
But trust…
What's coming is even better.

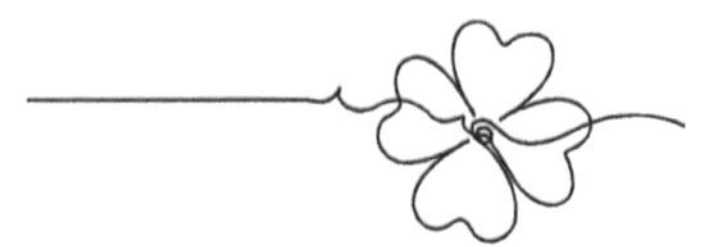

If you long for a simpler life,
Let your heart dance with a single focus at a
time.

If pain whispers through your soul—
Wrap yourself in the warmth of healing.
If joy sparkles in your eyes—
Let gratitude bloom like a thousand stars.
And if all feels still, like a quiet void—
Close your eyes…
Drift into the vastness of infinity,
Where dreams are born and magic quietly stirs.

The secret is this:
Don't chase the storm.
Follow the light.
Feel the magic.
Trust the whispers of the universe…
And focus on the solution

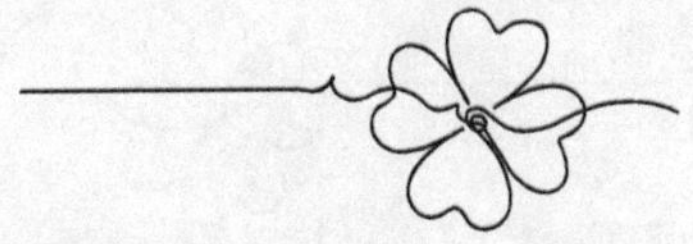

When every feeling swirls like stardust in your
soul,
Close your eyes… and reach for the love.
It's there—soft, glowing, timeless.
Pluck it gently, cradle it in your hands,
Whisper your dreams into its light,
And let it bloom a little more.

Now…
Drop it back into the cosmic dance of emotions.
Watch as it ripples through every shadow,
Turning pain into healing,
Fear into courage,
Silence into song.

Suddenly, everything shifts.
Everything glimmers.
Everything… is love.
Because love was always the secret,
Waiting to be found.

You're searching for the right one,
Trying to manifest with all your heart.
But here's a secret—
Manifestation isn't about chasing…
It's about loving.

Love the very thing you desire.
Breathe it. Live it. Become it.
Let its essence dance in your soul
Until the lines between longing and having
disappear.

Manifestation is not a chase—it's a surrender.
It's the art of believing so deeply,
Of feeling so completely,
That the universe has no choice
But to weave your dreams into reality.

You're not waiting for magic…
You *are* the magic.

Forgive…
Because your heart holds a magic stronger than
any pain.
Forgive…
So the winds of the universe can sweep away the
past,
Making room for stars to align in your favor.

Forgive…
Until your soul feels as light as stardust,
Until the whispers of peace dance through your
being.
And when life stirs the storm once more…
Forgive again.
And always.
For in forgiveness lies the secret to unlocking
miracles.

It's not too late—the stars are still singing your
name.
The universe whispers, "Begin again."
Not for them. Not for the world.
But for the magic that sleeps inside you.
Close your eyes and feel it—
A spark, gentle and ancient, waiting to rise.
Let your hidden desires dance like fireflies in the
night,
Casting light upon the path only your heart can
see.
Carry them into your dreams,
And when dawn caresses the sky,
Awaken with a soul reborn—
As if the universe itself conspired
To wrap you in courage and stardust,
Guiding you back to your truest self.
Today is a new spell,
A promise waiting to bloom.
Begin

Start small. Start messy. Start anywhere—but
start.
When tomorrow greets you, and the first stone
rests in place,
A gentle whisper will rise: "Keep building. Keep
dreaming."
But don't rush.
Let each step be a dance with destiny,
Each breath a quiet spell of creation.
Feel the magic in the unseen,
The way dreams softly weave into reality.
Every brick you lay is a promise to the
universe—
That you believe in the castle only you can build.
Stay in that wonder,
For magic blooms when you cherish
Every flicker of hope and every spark of courage.
Your castle is waiting.

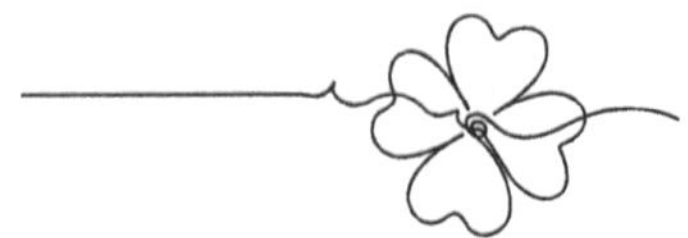

Magic, my love,
Is not just a metaphor—
It's the quiet knowing in a mother's eyes
Before words ever find their way.
It's the warmth of family, wrapped in laughter,
Where time slows, and hearts dance freely.
Magic is work that feels like play,
Dreams whispered on the wind,
And the secret art of cradling your emotions,
Knowing which ones need guarding
Before they greet the world.
Magic isn't distant—
It shimmers in every breath, every blink,
A soft touch against your soul.
Feel it.
Live it.
Let it show you the boundless joy
That has always been yours to hold.

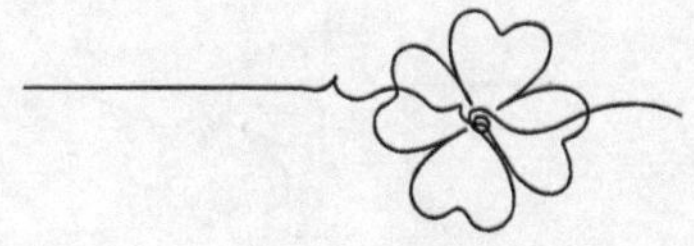

Whisper softly to your heart who you are,
Before the world tries to write its story on your
soul.
There is a quiet kind of magic in knowing
yourself—
A light that flickers softly at first,
But grows into a blazing fire when nurtured.
Perhaps you are a storm, fierce and unyielding.
Or maybe you are the dawn, gentle and full of
promise.
Whatever you are, discover it.
For when tomorrow arrives, and the world
stands before you—
Some seeking, some certain—
You will not waver.
You will shine.
A beacon of truth,
A soul who dared to find its own path
Before the stars whispered it into existence.

The world is a marketplace.
Have you heard that before?
Did you believe it?
If you did, then surely you've met some
merchants along the way,
And perhaps it broke your heart to realize that
not everyone cares.

But the world is also a beautiful place.
Have you heard that before?
If you believed that… oh, what stories you must
hold!
Stories of magic, of kindness, of love that
bloomed in the most unexpected corners.
If we ever meet, promise me this—
Tell me about the greatest love stories you
created
With nothing but faith and a heart wide open.
I'll be listening.

One holiday evening,
Take a book—the one that whispers to your soul.
Brew yourself a cup of warmth, or a chilled
potion if that soothes your spirit.
Close your eyes for a moment.
Feel your breath, soft and steady,
Like the tides of the ocean, rising and falling.
Then, gently turn the pages.
Even if it's just one…
Let the words wrap around you,
Like a secret spell meant only for you.
Just read—and let the magic unfold.

Childhood holds the best memories,
Not because time was kinder, but because we
were protected.
As we grow, that feeling fades, hidden beneath
layers of emotions and expectations.
But I know a secret—a protection charm.
Whisper these words to your heart:
"I am with you, always."
Now that you know you're never alone,
Create new memories, dance with wonder,
And let the child within you breathe freely once
more…
For it is safe. It is loved. It is protected.

I know that only I can navigate the curves of my life. Yet, I seek help, reaching out to external resources to make things work. Deep down, I understand that only I can heal my memories and create a better path forward.

Perhaps it's because I'm afraid to truly listen to myself. Not because I don't trust myself anymore, but because I'm afraid that if I do, I might begin to love myself again.

I think, in some way, I'm scared to love myself, fearing that I might hurt myself in the process. But this fear is just a surface belief. Deep within, I know that I am as good and pure as the soul I was born with.

Next time, I will take the courage to listen to myself. Slowly but surely, I will learn to love myself once more.

Okay?

Time heals, But only when we allow ourselves the space to listen to the whispers of our head, mind, and soul. Time can truly mend us only when we address the memories that cause us pain, allowing them to heal first.

Take the time to reflect. Take the time to strengthen the good memories and forgive yourself for the ones that are less so.

You are worthy of the love you once believed was beyond your reach.

Somewhere in the world, someone seems to
have it all, and you watch, wondering why such
wonders never found you. But perhaps their
secret lies in the way they love—effortlessly,
endlessly, pouring magic into every moment.
You can too. Love deeply, and watch the
universe unfold its miracles.

Beautiful creations are born when you honor
your magic, letting your soul dance with the
whispers of the universe and blossom like
stardust beneath a moonlit sky

This very moment holds a quiet magic—as wondrous as you dare to believe. So, if I whisper that something beautiful is on its way, and your heart listens, the universe will conspire to make it true.

Close your eyes... breathe... and feel it. Something wonderful is about to happen

Don't wait for someone to return—rise and create your own radiant comeback. Fill your world with light, whisper to your heart that you deserve the most beautiful things, and trust that what's meant for you will find its way back, like a star drawn to its sky. Believe that magic flows to those who shine kindness upon others, but most importantly, upon themselves.

Change the way you see yourself, and the world will awaken before you—unfolding like a dream, shimmering with magic and endless possibilities.

One degree higher with each new dawn, and
the universe guides you closer to your destined
brilliance. Each step, bathed in starlight, leads
you toward the final, radiant destination that's
been waiting for you all along.

The things you run from always seem to follow, as if bound to you by an unseen force, eager to linger. But if you simply stop, turn, and face them, you'll realize—they are but thoughts, and thoughts can be transformed. Don't raise your voice; speak gently instead. If they listen, release them with love. If they don't, listen closely, for they hold whispers meant to guide you. Learn, let go, and set yourself free

Step into the moment when the world feels
abundant, when every breath overflows with
more than enough—for in that radiant stillness,
you will find a freedom so deep, so boundless,
that it will set your soul to dance in the stars.

Centre yourself, for within your heart lies the quiet strength. When life spins out of control, let your thoughts return to that sacred place. For the heart holds a magic so gentle, it can melt even the fiercest storms, turning chaos into calm

You will do well in this life, and all that you've dreamed and worked for will be yours. But for now, focus on what you can give. The more you open your heart to give freely, the more the universe will open to receive your blessings. Choose wisely, for what you give will return to you in ways beyond imagining.

Gaze upon something beautiful, let your eyes
linger until you realize that everything around
you already hold its own magic. We often make
the journey harder than it needs to be, as if we
must struggle for the simplicity and ease that are
already ours, waiting patiently along our path

One day, when you look back, you will smile
at the moments you once thought were too
difficult to bear—the heartbreak, the dreams that
slipped away, the struggles no one else could
understand. Your life, in its quiet wisdom, knows
what's best for you. Sometimes, all you need to
do is surrender, allowing it to unfold the magical
beginnings meant just for you.

Sometimes, the magic lies in doing less—for
there is no need to try when everything is
already unfolding in its own time

Love will find its path, like a soft whisper carried by the wind, gently healing your heart and renewing your spirit. With each beat, it will awaken a new purpose within you, guiding your hands to create wonders that sparkle like hidden stars, waiting to light up your world.

Your creation is not meant to stay merely in
your mind; it must pass through the sacred
chamber of your heart. For the heart, my love, is
a mystical place where thoughts transform into
dreams, where the deepest of musings bloom
into the most extraordinary wonders, ready to
enchant the world.

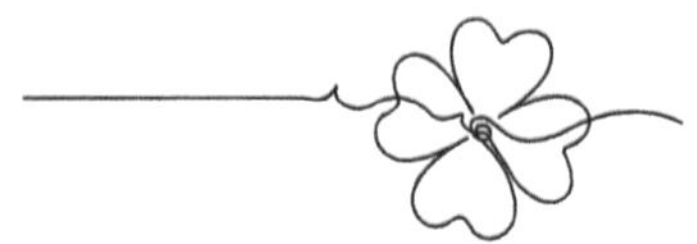

We long for someone to truly understand us,
Not for solutions, but simply to be seen.
Even if no answers are given,
The act of being understood is enough.
I understand you,
The quiet strength in every step you've taken,
And all that you are enduring.
I am here with you, always—
A constant light, beside you, through it all

*kabhi thak jaya karo, thak kar so jaya karo, khud ke
liye bematlab yuh waqt jaya kiya karo, tumhe khud se
pyaar hai, bas yahi kafi hai sab jatane ke liye*

Sometimes, let yourself feel the weight of
weariness,
And rest in the quiet embrace of your own soul.
Give yourself moments with no purpose,
Just for you, for the magic that lies within.
The love you hold for yourself—
That alone is enough to illuminate the world,
A soft glow that speaks louder than any words.

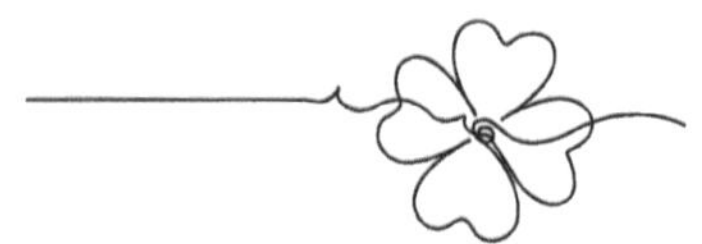

It will find its way to you, all that you've ever
dreamed of,
Everything you've poured your heart, soul, and
body into.
The only pause is in the belief you hold within,
The moment you trust that you were destined for
this,
You will see it was always written in the stars,
waiting for you to claim it,
As if the universe had been waiting for you to
awaken to your own magic

Do it for yourself, and for the world that dances around you. Heal, not just for your own soul, but for the unseen threads that connect you to countless lives, directly and indirectly. You are a beacon, shining without even knowing how many lives are touched by your light. Be the hero of your own story, for in your healing, you become the spark that awakens the magic in others

The power of your soul stirs only when you
choose to awaken it, when you truly call upon
its strength. When life begins to slip away,
surrender completely—for there is an infinite
force that has carried you this far. This force will
return to you what is destined, if it's meant for
this journey. If not, rest assured, something even
more wondrous awaits you, woven with the
magic of the universe

Laugh a little, smile a little, and finally learn to live for yourself. Release the hopes you've held tightly, let them spread their wings and fly. For hope, with its radiant power, transforms every challenge into a triumph, and fills your heart with victory, no matter the path

You often ask me, 'What will be my future?' I already know what will unfold for you. You will become everything your heart believes, once you lift every stone of doubt. If, deep within, you hear a voice telling you that the best is yet to come, trust it—because that's exactly what will manifest, brighter and more beautiful than you ever imagined.

Who says you must stay happy all day long?
If your heart feels weighed down, follow its
whispers. Dive deep into why it feels that way,
and ask yourself what you can do to ease it.
Trust with all your soul that everything will fall
into place—it will, and nothing else will matter,
for the universe has its way of making things
right

We set out in search of love, carrying with us a long list of dreams. But the greatest force in this universe doesn't need to see this list. If you seek love, first give love—begin with yourself. Fill your heart so fully, so beautifully, that when the right love comes, it will feel like destiny. And it will find you, effortlessly, as the universe dances in harmony with your heart

Thoughts aren't built in a day; they are shaped through conversations, through deep reflections, and by repeating the words that resonate within. Imagine that your life is changing, slowly but surely, and now believe that you can make it happen. On day one, it may seem uncertain, but after thirty days, you won't even have to think twice—you'll see it, right in front of you, unfolding beautifully.

If someone enters your life, welcome them
with warmth. If someone leaves, let them go
with love. Do you know where true peace and
strength come from in life? From understanding
yourself. The more deeply you connect with
your own soul, the more you grow, like a flower
reaching toward the sun—ever brighter, ever
more beautiful, as you embrace your own light

Why rush so much? Take a moment, pause. Go to
that corner of your mind where silence resides,
where everything is one with 'nothingness.'
Now, try to see—is what you're about to do truly
necessary? Look within, for sometimes the quiet
holds the greatest truth

I know that we all hold the knowledge within
us—it's the same wisdom in every one of us. Yet,
sometimes, it feels like someone needs to come
along and remind us of it. Not all at once, but
slowly, bit by bit, until we remember the truth
that has always been there, quietly waiting

Do you know what happens when courage shatters, faith breaks, and every corner of your heart feels scattered? A miracle. Because in this world, there is a force—of which we are but a part—and simply staying connected to it is the greatest feeling of all

Has anyone ever told you? That you carry magic within you, something so special that even you may not fully know it yet. There's a warmth, a beautiful essence, that everyone around you can feel just by being near you. You are unique, and deep down, you already know this. I just wanted to remind you.

People are stepping into their future! Writing new chapters of their lives! Exploring uncharted paths! Driving new dreams! Building connections that sparkle with possibility! So, my love, who's stopping you? Pause for a moment and reflect… The universe is unfolding, and it's waiting for you to embrace your magic.

Are you searching for something? Imagine you've already found it! Now, take one more step. Feel it, as if you've already achieved it. Just one more step. Now, let it come to you! There is no other option but for it to find its way to you. What is truly yours will always find its way back to you.

Have you ever witnessed a miracle? Truly? What
you are today, everything you've achieved—
these are all the miracles of your inner self. The
more you unravel the mysteries within, the more
they will rise and reveal themselves. Be thankful
for every small miracle in your life, for there
is no greater power in this universe than the
strength of a grateful heart.

There is a subtle difference between strength and power. Strength is soft, gentle, and infinite, while power seeks only to find softness. So, whenever an emotion stirs within, let it rise. It is clearing the path for grace to enter, for healing to unfold, and for your soul to bloom. Trust the flow, for it is creating space for the most divine magic to fill your being.

One day, just one day, give yourself the gift of alignment. Set a gentle target for yourself—to connect what is outside with what lies within. When both your inner world and outer world come into harmony, everything will begin to fall into place, and you'll realize the miracle that has quietly unfolded.

Have you ever heard that what you run from
will always chase you? Have you ever wondered
why that happens? Because, in running, your
mind keeps replaying that thought over and
over, turning it into a story that becomes the
truth of your life.
So, here's what you must do: stop, turn around,
and face it. It will come, maybe scream, maybe
shout, but don't be afraid. For now, you know
that there is a powerful force within you, always
with you. Look into its eyes, see what it truly
needs, and give it what it asks.
By doing this, you'll lose nothing—in fact, you'll
witness everything slowly coming together, and
in the process, you'll find yourself again.

My wish is for all your desires to come true, but
before that, become worthy of them. For when
you align with your true potential, the universe
will unfold everything you've ever dreamed of.

At the end of the day, our thoughts, our decisions, and our actions shape the world we live in. They hold the power to create our destiny. That's why, when you pause to reflect, when you take a moment to truly think, you unlock a deeper magic. It's in those quiet moments that the universe aligns with your intentions. Isn't it wonderful how much power you hold?

Stop running!
Pause for a moment.
Nothing is leaving.
What is yours, what is meant for you—it will
come, just as it is meant to.
Until then, stay still, create something new, and
be happy.
For in the stillness, magic unfolds.

Let's try a little hack to return to silence:
Bow your head low, and breathe deeply 500
times.
Let those emotions rise, but know this—you are
stronger than them.
Accept each one, forgive what needs to be
forgiven.
Let gratitude be your guiding light,
And allow yourself to heal.
In that space, let the magic flow freely.

For now, know this—this moment is the best thing that has happened. Try embracing a new feeling this time. Instead of dwelling on why things didn't work out, shift your focus to what could work out, to the possibilities that might be even better than what came before.

Sometimes, we don't know why things didn't work out, why something fell apart, or why someone walked away without a word. Allow yourself 10 days to heal—no more than that. Pick yourself up. I am with you every step of the way. Look at yourself in the mirror and be proud of how far you've come. Take a deep breath, start small, and become the best version of yourself. Remember to forgive, and let gratitude fill your heart. The magic is in your hands

The future you is patiently waiting for you to begin. Start by loving yourself, start by taking care of your well-being, and start with the smallest acts of kindness. In doing so, prosperity will follow, unfolding in ways you can't yet imagine.

You hold a beautiful tomorrow in your hands. Live in the present moment, for it is the doorway to infinite possibilities. Embrace the feeling of eternity, where time dances softly and all things are connected. This world is filled with wonders waiting to unfold. Shift your focus, open your heart, and align yourself with the receiving mode of miracles. Watch as the universe, with all its magic, begins to flow toward you in ways you've never dreamed.

Your creation is timeless, etched into the very soul of the universe. With every intention, every stroke of creativity, you are casting your essence into eternity. Choose wisely, for what you create today will ripple through the stars, shaping the infinite, dancing with the magic of the cosmos forever

Hope, and the words of inspiration, are your magical weapons—woven with the power to transform the impossible into the possible. Carry them with you, let them ignite your soul. With each step, the universe aligns, and excellence becomes not just an outcome, but your destiny

When the rain nourishes the earth, new sprouts
will stretch their wings toward the sky. Your
significance will remain ever true, timeless and
unchanging, a part of the universe's eternal
rhythm.

Take your palms, and kiss them with reverence.
The more love you infuse into your being, the
more your fortune will unfold, like a garden
blooming under the light of the stars, growing
with each act of love you sow.

If that path didn't work, try a new one. Anything you pour your energy into will flourish and return to you in ways more wondrous than you could ever imagine. Keep working, keep loving, and keep hoping—your efforts are being woven into something magnificent, just beyond the horizon.

Anything is as playful as you make it, and
as profound as the energy you infuse into
it. Embrace the mystery and the wonder of
the moment—when you choose to laugh, the
universe laughs with you. Have fun, for life itself
is a spell waiting to be cast!

You are limitless, with the power to focus on
the promise of a brighter tomorrow and craft
the most extraordinary life. You are already
free. Close your eyes, feel the boundless energy
within, and with all your will, take flight!

Freedom is a choice, my love. Your courage is the key to unlocking your will to be free. And courage is born from the acts of kindness you give—soft and hard are but metaphors. Your true identity lies in what you believe about yourself. Keep believing, and keep becoming.

One single feeling for the rest of your life

UNCONDITIONAL LOVE

Whether you realize it yet or not, you are a
beacon of luck, blessed with endless abundance
and prosperity. The universe has already woven
these gifts into your journey. Once you open
your heart to the truth that you deserve every
spark of this magic, it will flood your life in ways
beyond imagining.

Home… You are already home. This moment, right here, is the best moment, filled with endless possibilities. Your fortune has already been woven, beautifully and miraculously, into the fabric of your life. You are a blessed being, now and forever.

Don't try to figure it all out. Just sail. What you need to know will come to you, and everything you require for your journey will be led to your doorstep. If you want to create something, simply SURRENDER and have unwavering FAITH

The formless is the eternal creator, weaving the
fabric of your life with boundless energy and
infinite love. It holds the power to make you
free—carefree, joyful, and deeply connected to
the wonders of the universe. The formless is
always with you—its presence is in every breath
you take, protecting, providing, and enveloping
you in pure love. Though it may take on a
name in your heart, a shape in your soul, or a
face in your dreams, the formless is the source
from which we all emerge, eternally present,
shaping the world in ways beyond our knowing.
Surrender to this powerful force, let it guide you,
and feel the magic of life unfold with every step,
as love and light fill your every moment

Create a life ahead of your time, one that exists in the realm of dreams and limitless possibilities. Take a moment to lean into the feeling of a great day unfolding before you. Bask in that sensation, hold it close, and let it fill you with warmth and joy. Allow yourself to feel this bliss for as long as it takes to release the worries and embrace the magic of the moment. Know that every thought you have now is shaping the extraordinary day ahead.

Today, when you step out and face the sun,
know that something wondrous is awaiting
you. In the warmth of its light, you will meet
yourself—your truest, most powerful self—and
feel the magic flow into your life. Be brave, step
forward, and embrace the sunlight, for it holds
the key to the miracles unfolding for you. I know
you are ready, and the universe knows it too

I can't promise you the best life, but I know that every small act, every moment, will guide us toward one. Today, this very moment, is all you truly have. So be present in your own endeavour, allow yourself to dissolve into the oneness with the Supreme, and watch as the magic unfolds before you. Trust that each step you take is part of a grander design, and let yourself flow with it.

When all the doors seem to close, when no one
is listening, and nothing appears before you...
that's when something huge and beautiful is
about to unfold in your life. Ever tried to increase
the flow of water through a pipe? By closing
the outlet and applying pressure, the flow
intensifies. It's just like that now. Trust me, let
go of all your worries—there's a power at work,
even though you can't see it yet. It's helping you,
guiding you towards something magnificent.

Faith and belief don't reveal their full strength in a single moment. They begin to weave their magic the moment you start embracing them. You must reach a point of solitude, a space where the soul finds its own rhythm, where belief becomes natural, and where everything needed to keep you moving forward begins to unfold effortlessly. Keep going, trust the process—you're closer than you think

Karma is not fate; it is the strength that shapes your destiny. Every action, every intention, is a thread woven into the fabric of your life, creating the path that leads to your own creation.

Your energy centre, like your mind, need regular
cleansing to stay aligned. Between your two
eyes, just above the brow, lies a powerful centre
that helps declutter and clarify your thoughts.
When things don't seem to flow, it's often time to
give extra attention to this space, allowing clarity
to emerge and guide you back to your path.

Within you lies a power so deep, so infinite, that once awakened, it will shift the very fabric of your world. Every breath you take is an opportunity to create, to release, to step into the flow of the universe. Trust in the whispers of your soul, for it already knows the path. The more you believe in the magic that surrounds you, the more it reveals itself. All that you seek is already within your reach, waiting for you to claim it. Let go, trust, and watch as the universe begins to dance in harmony with your heart's desires

Your words are like seeds planted in the garden of your soul. With every positive thought, with every kind word you speak to yourself, you are nurturing a garden of infinite possibilities. Imagine each word as a spark, lighting the path towards your greatest desires. Believe in the magic within you, for it is woven into the very fabric of your being. When you speak, the universe listens and dances to the rhythm of your thoughts. Trust that your words will manifest the world you dream of. You are a creator, a magician in your own right, capable of transforming dreams into reality

You are born with the universe's blessing in every breath you take, a constant flow of luck running through you like a river of magic. There is no path but the one that leads to abundance and joy. Embrace the luck that's already yours, for it's your birthright. With every step, the world will unfold in your favor, and great things will find their way to you. All that you dream of is destined to be part of your reality. So, trust, savor, and allow the beauty of the world to embrace you

Mati ko ek beej dedo,
Wo pani khud dhoyega,
Khich suraj ko paas itne,
Wo khud naya jeevan boyega.

Mati ko ek beej dedo,
Wo sukoon se reh paayega,
Khud sich sich har kankar usse,
Fal bhi khud na khayega.

Mati ko ek beej dedo,
Wo saare halat se lad jayega,
Khud ki sahen shakti se,
Wo jad tak use sehlayega.

Mati ko ek beej dedo,
Wo sehensheel ban jayega,
Purv disha se pachim tak,
Wo har disha lehrayega.

Mati ko ek beej dedo,
Wo apne sapno ko poora karega,
Har mushkil ko apna banayega,
Aur ek nayi kahani ka aagaz karega.

Mati ko ek beej dedo,
Jo kabhi na thame, kabhi na roke,
Wo apni duniya khud banayega,
Mati ko ek beej dedo!

Take a deep breath, everything is fine,
I am with you,
Together, we will complete this journey,
I have your hand, and I will lead you forward.

If everything feels worthless right now, let it be,
If you feel like burning everything to ashes, do
so.
Let all those fears rise within,
So we know what we need to fight against.

This battle is not with yourself, nor with anyone
else,
This battle is simply with the thoughts of time
itself.
And time, with its tricks, will never tire you,
You will find your way by trusting your thoughts
and the path within.

I am with you, and together we will win.
Everything will blossom like flowers after the
rain,
Your life will turn into a beautiful journey, just
trust yourself

Self-acceptance and self-concept are not just companions, they are the keys to unlocking the vast, infinite magic within you. When you harmonize these energies within yourself, you align with the universe in ways that transcend understanding. You become a living manifestation of the miracles you've always sought. Imagine this: with every breath you take, every thought you choose to nurture, you create ripples of magic, shaping your reality in ways that seem impossible to others, but are nothing short of natural for you.

When you accept yourself fully, you step into
a flow so powerful that the world around
you transforms. Every challenge becomes an
opportunity, every setback a stepping stone.
The universe dances in rhythm with your soul,
guiding you to places and experiences beyond
your wildest dreams. Your life becomes a canvas,
painted with the hues of boundless possibility.
The only limit is the one you choose to set, and
even that, in your infinite wisdom, is meant to be
surpassed.

Trust in your power, trust in your journey, and
trust that miracles aren't just possible—they are
inevitable.

Attracting anything into your life requires more than just setting goals and boundaries; it requires a deep alignment within yourself. When you create, you must bring your mind, your effort, and your soul into harmony. These are the pillars of your existence, and when they work in unison, the universe responds with limitless possibilities.

Mind: Your thoughts shape your reality. It's not enough to think about your desires—you must believe in them with unwavering faith.

A focused, positive mind will attract the experiences, people, and opportunities that align with your vision. But it's not just about thinking; it's about being present, being aware of your thoughts, and choosing ones that uplift you.

Effort: Manifestation isn't passive. It requires action, even if those actions are small. Each step you take toward your goal is a message to the universe that you are ready. Action allows you to co-create with the universe, but it's important that your effort feels aligned, not forced. When you feel the effort is loving, gentle, and empowering, that's when it creates the most impact.

Soul: Your soul knows what is best for you. It whispers to you through your intuition, guiding you toward what you truly need. When you create from a place of soul-deep desire, it is infused with love and authenticity. Your soul will steer you toward what truly aligns with your essence. When your soul is involved, it's not about seeking approval from outside—it's about fulfilling your deeper purpose.

When you blend these three elements—mind, effort, and soul—you create a balance that not only attracts what you want but also aligns you with the abundance that the universe has in store. Your creation becomes an act of love, an act of flow, and from that space, miracles unfold effortlessly. So, yes, create everything that feels loving to you, and let that loving energy guide every step of your journey.

The beauty of life lies not in the final destination, but in the journey itself. The more we focus on enjoying each moment, embracing the lessons, and savoring the experiences, the more fulfilling life becomes. We often get caught up in the race to achieve, to win, but true joy comes when we allow ourselves to be present, to appreciate the small steps, and to learn from the ups and downs along the way.

When you shift your focus from just winning to truly living in the moment, the process itself becomes beautiful and magical. The journey teaches you more than any destination ever could. So, if we stop stressing over the end result and start finding joy in the now, life unfolds in ways we never imagined possible—more beautiful, more rewarding, and more aligned with who we are meant to be.

Exactly! The power of belief is the first step toward achieving anything you desire. When you truly believe that you can do something, that you are deserving of it, and that you already possess everything you need to make it happen, you unlock a limitless potential within yourself.

Belief isn't just about wishful thinking; it's about aligning your thoughts, actions, and energy with the outcome you want. Once you fully embrace that belief, the universe responds by bringing you opportunities, guidance, and the strength to move forward.

Remember, the only thing standing between you and your dreams is the belief that you can achieve them. Once you make that connection, everything else falls into place. You've already got everything you need. Just take that first step with confidence, and watch how everything unfolds!

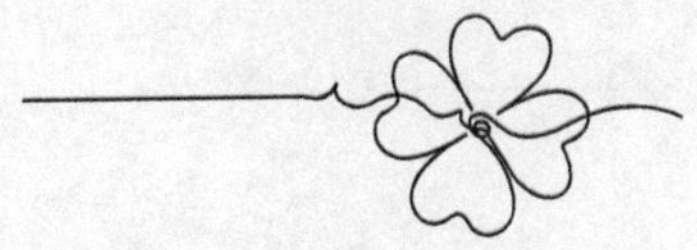

The power of small steps is often underestimated, but it's one of the most effective tools for achieving greatness. When something feels impossible, breaking it down into tiny, manageable actions allows you to stay focused and make consistent progress without feeling overwhelmed.

Each small step you take, no matter how tiny it seems, adds up over time. It creates momentum, builds your confidence, and allows you to gather strength with every action. The beauty of this approach is that it's sustainable—it doesn't require you to leap forward all at once. Instead, it's about steady, determined progress.

Remember, even the tallest mountains are climbed one step at a time. Each small effort compounds into something monumental, and soon you'll look back and realize how far you've come. Keep moving, even if it's just a little at a time. You'll be amazed at what you can achieve!

The moment you transcend the lens of illusion, you awaken to the realization that the power you seek has always been within you. That formless energy—often hidden behind the veil of doubt and distraction—shapes your thoughts and desires into tangible outcomes. It's when you align your mind, heart, and actions with this unseen force that miracles begin to unfold.

What once seemed impossible becomes a reality, not because the universe is granting you special favors, but because you have finally tapped into the boundless power within. This power is always at work, silently guiding and creating through your belief, effort, and focus.

When you stop looking at life through the lens
of limitation and begin seeing through the lens
of infinite possibility, the magic unfolds. Every
step, every thought, and every action becomes
infused with purpose. That's when your most
awaited miracles will begin to manifest—slowly,
but inevitably. Trust the process and keep
moving forward. The universe has its way of
surprising you in the most beautiful of ways

everything is aligning in your favor, even when it doesn't seem so. The energy, the "shakti," is constantly flowing, working in the background, weaving the threads of your dreams into reality. When you close your eyes and surrender, you're not giving up control, you're trusting the universe, trusting that this force is guiding you to where you need to be.

Let go of the need to figure everything out or control every detail. Allow the flow to carry you. Trust that the right things are happening at the right time. Even in the quiet moments, when it seems like nothing is moving, know that the universe is busy creating the most perfect opportunities for you.

Sometimes, the best thing to do is simply to
let things unfold, to let this divine energy
work its magic. And in doing so, you'll find
that everything you need will come to you
effortlessly. Keep trusting, keep surrendering,
and watch as the shakti unfolds the magic you've
been waiting for.

When you look back at your journey, you'll see that this time, you've taken the reins in your own hands. You've chosen to shape your destiny, trust your path, and create your own future. It's an empowering realization—realizing that you are the architect of your own life, and the courage you showed along the way has built a foundation stronger than ever before.

Take a moment to feel proud. Not just for the destination you're reaching, but for every step, every decision, and every ounce of growth you've put into it. The pride you'll feel will be a reflection of the strength you've always had within you.

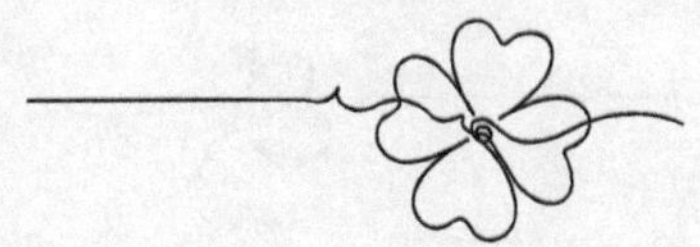

To truly achieve anything in life, understanding yourself is the first and most important step. When you take the time to talk to yourself, to reflect on your strengths, your dreams, and your potential, that's when you start to align with your true path. Praising yourself, recognizing your own worth, and accepting your journey are all essential to realizing your dreams.

Remember, when you recognize your own value, the world will reflect it back to you. The more you appreciate your unique qualities, the more the universe will conspire to bring you closer to what you truly deserve.

Time is abundant; what truly matters is how we
manage the space in our lives. When we learn
to prioritize, organize, and allocate our energy
wisely, everything falls into place effortlessly. It's
when we find balance in our thoughts, actions,
and intentions that life feels miraculous. This
is the magic of alignment, where everything
starts to flow smoothly and what once seemed
impossible becomes possible.

we all have a sacred space within us—a divine
place where our inner guidance resides. To reach
this place, we simply need to align our thoughts,
actions, and emotions with the divine energy
that flows through us. When we think, act, and
feel with purity and intention, we are drawn
closer to this divine presence, and everything we
need for our journey becomes clear. It's about
tuning into that inner wisdom and trusting the
process. You're already there, you just need to
embrace it fully.

Stop avoiding, face it with courage, embrace it with an open heart. Acceptance is the key to unlocking your freedom. Forgive, let go, and release the burden that's been holding you back. Once you do this, you'll find that you can finally run free—unburdened, unchained, and ready to embrace all the blessings that are waiting for you.

Let your words be like whispers of the universe, finely crafted with care, flowing effortlessly like the softest breeze. As you express your innermost thoughts, may each sentence carry a sense of grace, purpose, and clarity. Know that the magic lies not only in what you create but in how you create it—with intention, mindfulness, and love. Your journey is a work of art, each moment an opportunity to refine, to elevate, and to become the truest version of yourself. Trust that with each step, your inner light grows brighter, illuminating the path toward your dreams. You are both the artist and the masterpiece, unfolding with every breath.

The mind's power holds the key to transforming
dreams into reality. When you channel your
energy with intention, you become the architect
of your life. The moment you align your
thoughts, beliefs, and actions, the universe
unfolds pathways you never imagined. Embrace
stillness, listen to your inner wisdom, and
trust in your ability to create what you seek.
Your energy is a quiet force, but its impact is
profound, weaving the threads of possibility into
the fabric of your existence. The magic lies not in
what you wish for, but in what you believe you
can create.

Before conquering anything else, win over yourself first. Once you master your inner world, you will see how everything else falls into place with ease. When you hold power over your thoughts, your emotions, and your beliefs, the external challenges no longer feel so overwhelming. You become the creator of your own path, and with that mastery, the world around you responds in kind. Remember, the greatest victory is the one over yourself. ◎

There's a voice within that calls out to you, asking you to pause, to stay still, and to follow its guidance. Sometimes, it will lead you down dark paths, filling you with fear and uncertainty. But if you continue to follow it to the very end, you'll discover that the light you seek was always hidden in those shadows. The journey, though challenging, will lead you to a place of clarity, growth, and brilliance. Trust the process, for the light always shines brightest after the darkest of times.

To attract love, become the embodiment of love.
To invite happiness, radiate joy in every
moment.
This is the harmonious law of nature,
The more you align yourself with what you seek,
The universe will unfold it before you,
effortlessly.

Become the energy you wish to attract. The
essence you hold within will shape your world
in ways you cannot yet imagine

I know, deep within, that your heart is pure and your intentions are always good. You've always wished well for others, and because of that, the universe will shower you with blessings in ways you can't yet imagine. Your kindness is like a beacon, guiding positive energy and love your way.

Trust the process, for everything that is meant for you will find its way to you, gently and beautifully. The good you put into the world will come back to you in abundance, and the light you carry will only grow stronger. Keep believing in yourself, and watch the magic unfold.

When alignment meets magic, everything falls
into place. So, focus on aligning yourself with
your true purpose, your inner desires, and
your heart's deepest wishes. When you are in
harmony with yourself, you'll discover that
everything becomes possible—nothing will seem
out of reach.

Believe in your ability to create the life you
desire, and watch as the universe conspires to
make it happen. The power lies within you,
and once you align with it, magic will unfold
effortlessly.

There will be days when it feels like everything you've done, every thought you've had, and every effort you've put in seems lost. You may find yourself questioning it all, wondering why things aren't working out as expected. There may even be a storm outside, and the world may feel heavy and cold. But know this: every single thing you've ever created or felt is making its way back to you. It may not come in the form you envisioned, but it will arrive in a way that's even better than you imagined.

Keep your heart open, keep thinking, keep creating. The universe has a beautiful way of surprising us when we least expect it, transforming what we've built into something even more magnificent.

Write. Let your words flow like a energy, unrestricted and free. What you write holds more power than you can imagine. Each sentence you create carries a piece of your soul, a fragment of your essence that resonates in ways you can't always see or understand. It has the ability to transform, to heal, to inspire, and to manifest.

Writing is a bridge between your inner world and the universe, a direct line from your heart to the stars. It's a tool that holds magic—the kind that moves mountains, shifts perspectives, and sparks revolutions in quiet moments. So write, and trust in the strength of your words. They are more powerful than you think.

Show the courage to stand tall, be brave enough to face the challenges that come your way, and carry within you the strength to fight for what you believe is right for you. Have a vision, a plan that stretches beyond the immediate, one that sees the bigger picture—a plan that honors your journey and reflects your deepest values.

At the end of it all, remember this: the only thing that truly matters is the effort you put in, the positive energy you invest. Your commitment to what's right will create ripples that extend far beyond the present moment. Stay steadfast, and let your courage be your guide. The universe rewards the brave, the ones who keep pushing forward with unwavering belief.

Apni kahani apne haath se likho, har shabda tumhara apna ho, har mod tumhara khud ka faisla ho. Chhoti shuruwaat bhale hi ho, lekin apni neev ko humesha majboot rakho, kyunki wahi tumhe zindagi ke har mod par sambhal kar rakhne wali hai. Tumhara hausla, tumhara iraada hi tumhari kahani ka asli jadoo hai. Har kadam par apni taqat ko pehchano, aur apni zindagi ko apne sapno ke hisaab se rachne do

www.ingramcontent.com/pod-product-compliance
Lightning Source LLC
Chambersburg PA
CBHW030858120726
48008CB00002B/37